Powerful Polar Bears

Charlotte Guillain

Chicago, Illinois

© 2013 Raintree
an imprint of Capstone Global Library, LLC
Chicago, Illinois

Edited by Daniel Nunn, Rebecca Rissman,
and Catherine Veitch
Designed by Victoria Allen
Picture research by Mica Brancic
Production by Victoria Fitzgerald
Originated by Capstone Global Library Ltd

Library of Congress Cataloging-in-Publication Data
Guillain, Charlotte.
  Powerful polar bears / Charlotte Guillain.
    pages cm.—(Walk on the wild side)
  Includes bibliographical references and index.
  ISBN 978-1-4109-5218-9 (hb)
  ISBN 978-1-4109-5225-7 (pb)
  1. Polar bear—Juvenile literature. I. Title.
  QL737.C27G855 2013
  599.786—dc23   2012034700

Acknowledgments
FLPA: Dickie Duckett, Cover; Getty Images: All Canada
Photos/Don Johnston, 13, All Canada Photos/Ron Erwin,
29, Fred Bruemmer, 20, Mike Hill, 28, Oxford Scientific/
Daniel Cox, 12; Nature Picture Library: Andy Rouse, 7,
24, Eric Baccega, 23, Mats Forsberg, 17, Nick Garbutt,
22, Staffan Widstrand, 14, Steven Kazlowski, 8, 9, 10,
11, 16, 18, 21, 27; Shutterstock: Hal Brindley, 5, Sergey
Uryadnikov, 25, 26, Thomas Barrat, 19, Vlad Ghiea, 15,
Yvonne Pijnenburg-Schonewille, 4

We would like to thank Michael Bright for his invaluable
help in the preparation of this book.

Every effort has been made to contact copyright holders
of material reproduced in this book. Any omissions will
be rectified in subsequent printings if notice is given to
the publisher.

All the Internet addresses (URLs) given in this book were
valid at the time of going to press. However, due to the
dynamic nature of the Internet, some addresses may
have changed, or sites may have changed or ceased to
exist since publication. While the author and publisher
regret any inconvenience this may cause readers, no
responsibility for any such changes can be accepted by
either the author or the publisher.

Some words are shown in bold, **like this**. You can find
out what they mean by looking in the glossary.

Contents

Introducing Polar Bears

Polar bears are huge bears that look white and live in the **Arctic**. They are deadly hunters but are also very beautiful. Polar bears are the largest **carnivores** living on land.

Polar bears spend time both on land and in the sea.

Did you know?

The polar bear's Latin name, *Ursus maritimus*, means "sea bear."

Where Do Polar Bears Live?

The polar bear's **habitat** includes frozen sea ice, as well as land in the **Arctic** region.

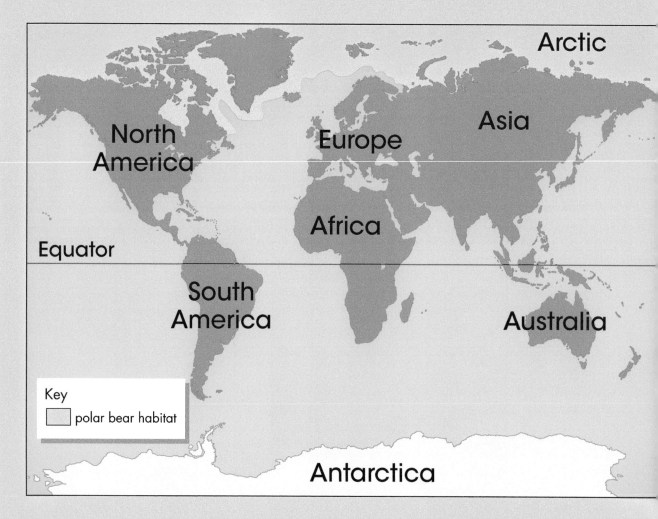

Arctic

North America

Europe

Asia

Africa

Equator

South America

Australia

Key
polar bear habitat

Antarctica

What Do Polar Bears Look Like?

Polar bears stand out because of their huge size and fur that looks white. They can be 10 feet long and weigh up to 1,500 pounds. Polar bears have long necks with fairly small heads. Their claws are curved and very strong.

Polar bears' teeth and claws are extremely sharp.

Fur and Skin

Polar bears' fur is **water repellent**. This means water does not stay in the fur and freeze. Under the fur is a thick layer of fat, which also keeps the bear warm. The skin under a polar bear's fur is black. Black skin holds any heat from the sun better than paler skin.

black skin

Polar Bear Paws

Polar bears' paws are specially **adapted** for life in the **Arctic**. Fur on the bottom of each paw helps to grip onto the ice as the bear moves around. A polar bear's huge paws help to stop it from sinking into the snow.

Getting Around

Polar bears cover huge distances looking for **prey**. They often walk around 20 miles in a day. Polar bears are also very good swimmers. Their front paws are partly **webbed** to help them swim. They can close their nostrils underwater.

Did you know?

Polar bears can swim for over 60 miles without stopping.

Hunting

Apart from females with cubs, most polar bears live and hunt alone. Their fur is good **camouflage** as they hunt on the ice. Polar bears use their camouflage to **stalk prey** without being seen.

Can you spot the polar bear?

seal pup

Did you know?

Polar bears mainly hunt seals, but they will also eat birds, walruses, and whales.

Super Senses

Polar bears use their excellent sense of smell to find **prey**. They can smell seals from more than 20 miles away. Polar bears also have good senses of sight and hearing.

Polar bears can smell
a seal's den under
thick ice.

Lying in Wait

When a polar bear has sniffed out a seal, it often waits near cracks or holes in the ice. When the seal comes up to breathe, the polar bear pounces.

Did you know?

Sometimes polar bears smash holes in the ice to find seal pups underneath.

Scavenging

When the sea ice melts in summer, it is harder for polar bears to hunt seals. Then they **scavenge** to survive. Polar bears will eat dead animals if they find them. They will also raid garbage cans in towns.

Polar bears eat berries in the fall.

It can be dangerous for people when polar bears look for food in towns.

Polar Bear Cubs

Female polar bears dig dens deep in the snow to give birth to cubs in the winter. The cubs drink their mother's milk, which is rich in fat. Cubs normally stay with their mother for over two years.

Did you know?

Polar bear mothers normally have twins.

Cubs leave the den in March or April.

Learning to Swim and Hunt

Mother polar bears teach their cubs how to hunt. At first the cubs watch. When they are about one year old, they start to hunt on their own. Mother bears also teach cubs how to swim. Sometimes mothers carry cubs on their backs if they have a long way to swim.

Life for a Polar Bear

Today, polar bears sometimes struggle to find food, because the sea ice in the **Arctic** is melting. It is important that humans protect their **habitat**.

Polar bears might look cute. But remember that they are some of the world's deadliest **predators**!

Glossary

adapted developed to suit the environment

Arctic polar region in the far north

camouflage coloring or disguise that hides an animal from view

carnivore meat-eater

habitat natural home for an animal or plant

predator animal that kills and eats other animals

prey animal killed by another animal for food

scavenge look for dead animals or garbage for food

stalk creep up on

water repellent does not soak up water

webbed having skin between toes to act as a paddle when swimming

Find Out More

Books

Ganeri, Anita. *The Polar Regions' Most Amazing Animals* (Animal Top Tens). Chicago: Raintree, 2008.

Meinking, Mary. *Polar Bear vs. Seal* (Predator vs. Prey). Chicago: Raintree, 2011.

Rosing, Norbert, and Elizabeth Carney. *Face to Face with Polar Bears* (Face to Face with Animals). Washington, D.C.: National Geographic, 2007.

Royston, Angela. *Polar Bears and Their Homes* (First Facts: The Big Picture). Mankato, Minn.: Capstone, 2010.

Web sites

Facthound offers a safe, fun way to find web sites related to this book. All the sites on Facthound have been researched by our staff.

Here's all you do:
Visit **www.facthound.com**
Type in this code: 9781410952189

Index